Colorful World of Animals

Green Tree Pythons

by Cecilia Pinto McCarthy

Consulting Editor: Gail Saunders-Smith, PhD

Consultant: Robert T. Mason, Professor of Zoology
J.C. Braly Curator of Vertebrates
Oregon State University
Corvallis, Oregon

CAPSTONE PRESS
a capstone imprint

Pebble Plus is published by Capstone Press,
151 Good Counsel Drive, P.O. Box 669, Mankato, Minnesota 56002.
www.capstonepub.com

Books published by Capstone Press are manufactured with paper
containing at least 10 percent post-consumer waste.

Library of Congress Cataloging-in-Publication Data
Cataloging-in-publication information is on file with the Library of Congress.
ISBN 978-1-4296-6052-5 (library binding)

Editorial Credits
Kristen Mohn, editor; Ted Williams, designer; Svetlana Zhurkin, media researcher; Laura Manthe, production specialist

Photo Credits
Getty Images/Carol Farneti Foster, 16–17
National Geographic Stock/Minden Pictures/FN/Otto Plantema, 4–5
Newscom/Danita Delimont Photography/Stuart Westmorland, 12–13
Photo Researchers/B. G. Thomson, 8–9
Photolibrary/Alan Root, 7; J-L. Klein & M-L. Hubert, 11
Shutterstock/Audrey Snider-Bell, 19; Reinhold Leitner, 20–21; Sergei Chumakov, 1; Stefan Simmerl, cover; Timothy
    Craig Lubcke, 15

Note to Parents and Teachers

The Colorful World of Animals series supports national science standards related to life science.
This book describes and illustrates green tree pythons. The images support early readers in
understanding the text. The repetition of words and phrases helps early readers learn new
words. This book also introduces early readers to subject-specific vocabulary words, which are
defined in the Glossary section. Early readers may need assistance to read some words and to
use the Table of Contents, Glossary, Read More, Internet Sites, and Index sections of the book.

Printed in the United States of America in North Mankato, Minnesota.
032011
006110CGF11

Table of Contents

Green Tree Snakes

Green tree pythons spend their days coiled in trees, waiting for an animal to come close. These snakes hide easily among tree leaves and vines.

Green tree pythons live in rain forests. They are found in northeast Australia, New Guinea, and nearby islands. These reptiles thrive in warm, wet weather.

where green tree pythons live

North America

Europe

Asia

Africa

South America

Australia

Antarctica

Long, Strong Bodies

Green tree pythons are

covered with smooth scales.

A strong tail grasps branches.

Pythons grow 5 to 7 feet

(1.5 to 2.1 meters) long.

A Tricky Hunter

To catch prey, a green tree python

wiggles the dark tip of its tail.

When an animal comes close,

the python catches it

with sharp front teeth.

The Big Squeeze

Pythons wrap around their prey
and squeeze to kill it.
Then they swallow
the prey whole.

After a big meal,

a green tree python may

not eat for 10 to 14 days.

Small mammals and lizards are

pythons' favorite foods.

Hatching and Growing

Female green tree pythons
lay six to 32 eggs. The mother
snakes coil around the eggs
and shiver to warm them.
In two months, babies hatch.

Python babies are red,

yellow, or brown. The babies

hide near the ground.

Their colors blend in

with the flowers and dirt.

After a year, the baby snakes have turned green. They move into the leafy canopy. Green tree pythons live 15 years or more.

Glossary

canopy—the middle layer of the rain forest where the greenery is thick and there is little sunlight

coil—to wind or wrap around something

hatch—to break out of an egg

mammal—a warm-blooded animal that breathes air; mammals have hair or fur

prey—an animal hunted by another animal for food

reptile—a cold-blooded animal that breathes air and has a backbone; most reptiles have scales

scale—one of the small pieces of hard skin covering the body of reptiles

shiver—to tremble

thrive—to live well and grow easily

Read More

Fiedler, Julie. *Pythons.* Scary Snakes. New York: PowerKids Press, 2008.

Rake, Jody Sullivan. *Pythons.* African Animals. Mankato, Minn: Capstone Press, 2008.

Sexton, Colleen. *Pythons.* Blastoff! Readers: Snakes Alive! Minneapolis: Bellwether Media, 2010.

Internet Sites

FactHound offers a safe, fun way to find Internet sites related to this book. All of the sites on FactHound have been researched by our staff.

Here's all you do:

Visit *www.facthound.com*

Type in this code: 9781429660525

Check out projects, games and lots more at
www.capstonekids.com

Index

Word Count: 212

Grade: 1

Early-Intervention Level: 19